The Extraordinary Gertrude Bell

Edited by Mark Jackson and Andrew Parkin

The Extraordinary Gertrude Bell

Obituary

Gertrude Lowthian Bell

The death of Miss Gertrude Bell at Baghdad on July 11 last, closed a career which in more than one respect is unique. No other woman of recent time has combined her qualities – her taste for arduous and dangerous adventure with her scientific interest and knowledge, her competence in archaeology and art, her distinguished literary gift, her sympathy for all sorts and conditions of men, her political insight and appreciation of human values, her masculine vigour, hard common sense and practical efficiency – all tempered by feminine charm and most romantic spirit. She was, I believe, the only woman to be graded a Political Officer during the Great War, and the only one after it to be Oriental Secretary to a High Commissioner. Not given to any sort of self-advertisement, she escaped, thanks to a lifelong indifference to what are called Feminist Movements, that advertisement by others which some distinguished members of her sex have suffered.

Obituary of Gertrude Bell written by D.G. Hogarth, *The Geographical Journal*, 68, 1926

Acknowledgements

There are several organisations to thank for the support they have provided in the production of this volume. They are the Great North Museum, the National Trust, Newcastle University and Tyne and Wear Archives and Museums. The editors are also indebted to a number of individuals who have helped during the publication process; we would like to thank Carlota González Míguez, David Hepworth, Sarah Glynn, Alex Boyd, Elizabeth Garnett and Vicky Manolopoulou. Finally we would like to thank all of the individuals who contributed their expertise to this volume, producing a wide-ranging set of papers that illustrate some of the many facets of Gertrude Bell's extraordinary life.

© Tyne Bridge Publishing, 2015

ISBN: 9781857951622

Published by:
City of Newcastle Upon Tyne
Newcastle Libraries
Tyne Bridge Publishing, 2015
www.tynebridgepublishing.co.uk

Design: David Hepworth

Right: *Ur of the Chaldees. View of Ziggurat from a distance (November 1916).*

Contents

Introduction

Gertrude Bell (1868 – 1926) is a key figure in the shaping of the Middle East in the early twentieth century. She played a major role in the establishment of the state of Iraq and was widely regarded as the foremost British expert on the region in the period immediately following the First World War. Her 1920 White Paper, *Review of the Civil Administration of Mesopotamia,* is an essential document for understanding British policy in the region. Yet, over time, her contribution has been overshadowed by others, in particular T.E. Lawrence (Lawrence of Arabia), who arguably did not have such a significant impact. More recent events in the Middle East following the Coalition invasion of Iraq in 2003 have led to renewed interest in Bell's career and her influence on the political map of the region.

Any examination of Bell's life reveals a complex individual whose political work in the Middle East was only one facet of a remarkable career. Born into an influential and wealthy family in the North East of England she was academically gifted, becoming the first woman to gain a first class honours degree in modern history from Oxford University. After Oxford she devoted much of her time to travel and writing, making extensive trips through Europe as well as spending several months in Tehran and taking two round the world tours. She also wrote about her experiences in Persia (*Persian Pictures*) and produced a critically acclaimed translation of the Persian poet Hafiz (*Poems from the Divan of Hafiz*). In addition she built up a formidable reputation as a mountaineer pioneering a number of challenging climbs in the Alps between the years 1899 – 1904.

By the turn of the Century, Bell was increasingly drawn to the Middle East and spent a great deal of time there travelling and exploring archaeological sites. In the years leading up to the First World War she immersed herself in the region, becoming fluent in Arabic as well as developing a deep understanding of the cultural and political life of the desert tribes. She published several books on her travels in the region, as well as important archaeological work on the Byzantine churches at Binbirkillise in Turkey (*The Thousand and One Churches*) and the Islamic palace at Ukhaidir (*Palace and Mosque at*

Ukhaidir: a Study in Early Mohammedan Architecture). Her intimate knowledge of the region led to her recruitment by British Intelligence during the First World War. She worked for the Arab Bureau in Cairo, producing reports on the desert tribes, later she was transferred to Iraq to carry out similar work. Her subsequent role in the post war creation of the state of Iraq was largely due to her war work and the important political connections she made. Towards the end of her life, as her political role waned, Bell returned to her love of archaeology, drafting Iraq's antiquities legislation and establishing the National museum in Baghdad.

Bell's intellectual and political achievements are testimony to her ambition, drive and ability. Nonetheless her personal life was marred by unhappiness and she possibly immersed herself in ambitious desert journeys or other work as a means of escape from this. During the course of her life she formed close relationships with a number of men, but none of these led to the settled married life she seemed to desire. She had wanted to marry Henry Cadogan, an official from the British embassy, who she met in Tehran. However her father refused to give his permission for this marriage and Bell, as a dutiful daughter, obeyed his wishes. In later life she was very close to the British soldier and diplomat Charles Doughty-Wylie, who was known to his friends as 'Dick'. Doughty-Wylie was already married when Gertrude met him; he was killed at Gallipoli in 1915. This doomed relationship caused her a great deal of sadness.

Gertrude Bell's life was a rich and varied one and this is reflected in the essays in this book which cover different aspects of her life and legacy. The volume complements Newcastle University's Gertrude Bell archive which houses her correspondence, letters and photographs, as well as her personal library, and comprises an invaluable resource for understanding her life and achievements. In addition it stands alongside an exhibition dedicated to Bell entitled '*The Extraordinary Gertrude Bell*', hosted by the Great North Museum: Hancock in Newcastle upon Tyne.

Andrew Parkin

The Iron-master's Daughter

Gertrude Bell is said to have opposed the Suffragettes' cause, 'votes for women'. Yet in one particularly important respect she espoused the same aims: Gertrude believed that women had as much right as men to choose the direction their lives should take, a commitment she expressed in her own life.

Gertrude Bell was not the only incredibly determined woman to have been born into the remarkably enlightened society which had emerged in the North East of England in the late seventeenth-century and which flourished throughout the eighteenth and nineteenth centuries. Recent research places Bell within this, much longer tradition, where independently-minded women inherited an experience of life uniquely related to Britain's industrial revolution.

The North East's archives contain a wealth of evidence relating to women similar to Gertrude Bell: women who owned land, property, coal, lead and many other valuable minerals, in the reign of Elizabeth I and continuously thereafter. These 'daughters of industry' inherited the same capital assets as sons, at a time when so many heirs did not survive childhood. It was therefore vital that the wealth accumulated by these families could be bequeathed through the female line: accordingly, families drew up separate legal contracts to protect women's wealth, particularly that of wives, since English law continued to deem husbands the rightful owners of their wives' assets.

By the time that Gertrude Bell was born, unmarried women controlled their own wealth. The fact that they were still not allowed to vote, a right denied to married and unmarried women alike, did not mean that they did not have a certain amount of choice over their own lifestyles. And, for middle class women like Gertrude Bell, whose family was directly responsible for achieving industrial progress, the opportunities for women to contribute to society had widened.

As the daughter, grand-daughter and great grand-daughter of three innovative ironmasters, Hugh, Isaac Lowthian and Thomas Bell, Gertrude Bell inherited wealth and a profound respect for it. Aged eight, she wrote of her excitement when visiting the family's 'Works', their iron foundries at Port Clarence, on the edge of the region's newest industrial town, Middlesbrough. Gertrude's father supervised her education for the next

play a very valuable role in family enterprises. The Quaker Darbys of Coalbrookdale encouraged their daughters to follow a spiritual 'calling', which many of them did as ministers, whilst others managed their family businesses. Daughters in such families were eminently well equipped to manage those businesses. Sarah Darby, her sisters and sisters-in-law, duly managed their family's iron founding Company during the Napoleonic Wars, as the widow, Theodosia Crowley, a third-generation industrialist, did: Theodosia managed the Crowley's Winlaton manufactory

seven years, until she went to a boarding school in London at fifteen: he imbued a respect for industry traditionally reserved for male heirs, in his gifted daughter.

British industrialists were amongst the most enlightened of parents when it came to educating their daughters. Though some historians have focussed on the extent to which marriage between the eighteenth and twentieth centuries was regarded as a fortuitous business arrangement, it is clear that intermarriage between *enterprising* families allowed ironmasters' daughters to

Top: *A wooden panel from a fireplace from the Bell family home of Rounton Grange near Northallerton in North Yorkshire. The panel refers to the family name and the importance of the family business of iron working.* © *The National Trust.*
Bottom right: *Gertrude and Sir Hugh Bell at Ziza in Iraq. This photograph was taken during Sir Hugh's second visit to Iraq in 1922.*

with the help of her two daughters for fifty-four years. She was regarded as an exemplary employer.

Gertrude Bell's parents believed she should be educated according to her own abilities. Gertrude therefore received the same sort of education which aristocratic women like Elizabeth Montagu, the north eastern coal-owner, London society hostess and 'Bluestocking', received, an education which prepared them not merely for an 'advantageous' marriage but for a life less ordinary than the majority of women, as female industrialists. Whilst this included learning ancient and modern languages, and about other cultures, this was also an ideal preparation for women who would go on to play an important role in business in male-dominated societies. Girls like Gertrude Bell, who received this sort of education, the daughter's equivalent of a son's 'Grand Tour' often found themselves destined to play a part in a larger society than their own. Bell, who described herself as an 'adventurous' child who relished talking to 'interesting people', acquired exactly the kind of education which prepared her for the role she was destined to play as a diplomat.

Whilst Gertrude Bell did not achieve the family life she so desired, she fulfilled other personal ambitions, as an adventurer and a respected ambassador, which were regarded as unfamiliar amongst women, by other women. Bell experienced 'opposition and suspicion' from women who judged her inferior on the grounds of her 'trade' inheritance. One pretentious aristocrat, Emily Lorimer, disdained Bell's inheritance because it had been acquired in 'scrap iron *or something*', which reminds us that, despite her family's importance in the North East, Gertrude Bell was considered an 'inferior' as far as Britain's land-owning class was concerned.

The remarkable Gertrude Bell emerges from this analysis as the rightful heir to a dynasty of enterprising north eastern women, the descendant of several equally-distinguished women, including her stepmother, Lady Florence Bell, who wrote one of the first social histories of an industrial population employed at the Bell's Middlesbrough 'Works'. Lady Bell's innovative description of the lives of the ironworkers' wives, which she regarded as 'a consolation and an example' to other women, and her admiration for their patience and fortitude, exemplified her position as a philanthropic employer. Yet they also show a genuine desire to understand the condition of the labouring class in the region, echoing what Gertrude Bell was to write concerning the lives of the Middle Easterners she encountered. Gertrude expressed the same respect for the less fortunate.

It remains incongruous that, as far as the British state politics was concerned, the pioneering Gertrude Bell was no more deserving than other women considered too irrational to vote.

This reminds us that, even in the first two decades of the twentieth century, educated, scholarly, adventurous and creative women like Gertrude Bell were in a minority. Yet Gertrude's achievements paralleled the Suffragettes' campaigns.

Not long after Gertrude died, in 1926, Nancy Astor won a seat in Britain's Parliament, the first female MP and, by all accounts, as 'formidable' a woman as Gertrude Bell had been.

Susan Beaumont

Right: *Gertrude Bell aged three, soon after the death of her mother in 1871.*
Below: *Gertrude, aged eight, with her father Sir Hugh Bell. Portrait by Edward Poynter.*

Gertrude Bell's Childhood Reading

Writing from Persia (modern-day Iran) to her cousin Horace Marshall in June 1892, Gertrude Bell offers evocative descriptions of her surroundings, commenting delightedly: 'Isn't it all charmingly like the *Arabian Nights*! but that is the charm of it all and it has none of it changed'. This remark not only draws heavily on popular Western cultural interpretations of the Middle East that depicted the area as charming, spiritual and timeless, but also reveals the extent to which her own understandings and perceptions of the area were influenced by literature. Not only do Gertrude's letters and diaries from her childhood and adolescence reveal her to be a voracious reader, devouring books from an early age, but they also demonstrate the impact of literature upon her love of travel and history.

The earliest record of Gertrude's love of books comes in a diary entry from November 1877, when she was just nine years of age, in which she writes that her stepmother had read to her 'a very amusing little book called *The Little Savage*'. The novel, written by Captain Frederick Maryatt, a Royal Navy officer and author of naval stories, was published in 1848, and tells the tale of a young English boy born on a remote South American island who then travels back to England. Also a firm childhood favourite with Gertrude was *Swiss Family Robinson* (1812), Johann David Wyss's tale of one family's shipwreck upon, and subsequent exploration of, a tropical desert island. Both narratives of adventure, these novels gave Gertrude her earliest tastes of the thrill of travel.

Along with such stories of adventure and exploration, Gertrude was also fascinated by historical fact and fiction, such as Grace Aguilar's 1852 novel, *The Days of Bruce: A Story from Scottish History*, which charted the life of King Robert the Bruce, who led the country in the first War of Scottish Independence against England. Gertrude relished learning about historical figures and events, and frequently read biographical works and collections of letters, including *Mozart's Letters*, *The Life of Macaulay* (Thomas Babington Macaulay, a historian and politician), and *A Catechism of Classical Biography: Containing an Account of the Lives of the Most Celebrated Characters among the Ancient Greeks and Romans*. However, amongst the factual accounts of lives, Gertrude also enjoyed a good, embellished tale of gore, writing to her stepmother in August 1881 that, 'I have been reading a very nice book belonging to Horace called *The Tower of London*; which Uncle Tom bought second-hand for 5s. and which he afterwards found was worth £5. It is all full of murders and tortures'. The book in question was *The Tower of London: A Historical Romance* (1840), by William Harrison Ainsworth, which centres on the character of Lady Jane Grey following her entrance to the Tower of London in July 1553.

In November 1884, Gertrude read Thomas Carlyle's 1836 comic novel, *Sartor Resartus*, which, through its central character Diogenes Teufelsdröckh, a fictional German philosopher, loosely parodied the work of Hegel. Gertrude wrote to her stepmother that 'I can't tell you how much I like *Sartor Resartus*, much better than any of the other books of his which I have read. I don't think I understand nearly all of it, however quite enough to show me how splendid it is. I think it gives me hundreds of new ideas; things which one had never dreamt of before. I shall read some more Carlyle soon'. Gertrude became a firm fan of Carlyle, reading both his account of the life of *Frederick the Great* (1858-65), and *Oliver Cromwell's*

Letters and Speeches, with elucidations by Carlyle (1845). A great admirer of Carlyle's writing, she occasionally sought to emulate his style, writing to her parents in November 1885 that 'The next letter I write to you, when I am not too cross to bother myself with finding words, my adjectives shall be as numerous and as expressive as Carlyle's own'. Gertrude was passionate about history, and was often incredibly affected by the accounts that she read. One book that particularly moved her was Dr John Doran's *London in the Jacobite Times* (1877), about which she wrote to her stepmother in November 1885: 'I've been dreadfully harrowed this morning by reading a book called *London in Jacobite Times*. It is so sad the way all those good, really excellent, and brave men threw away their lives for those despicable, worthless, faithless Stuarts. Oh! if anybody deserves fire and brimstone I'm sure the Stuarts do. I think one of the most miserable things on the face of the earth is to see good men throw themselves heart and soul and with the purest motives on the side of a wrong and bad cause. I could really cry over the bare story of Lord Derwentwater and some others which I read this morning'. Gertrude's love of history, fuelled by these and the many other books that she read during her childhood and adolescence, led to her taking a place at Oxford University to study History at Lady Margaret's Hall at the age of seventeen. Two years later, in June 1888, Gertrude became the first woman to be awarded a First in Modern History from Oxford. Her fascination for history also underpinned her love of archaeology, a love that took her across the Middle East on archaeological expeditions, and which endowed her with her in-depth knowledge of the area and its people.

Emma Short

Red Barns, Redcar. Gertrude's childhood home, designed by the noted arts and crafts architect Philip Webb.

A North-East Woman of Contradictions

Born at Washington Hall, County Durham in 1868, Gertrude Lowthian Bell was the daughter of Sir Hugh Lowthian Bell, the iron master of Middlesbrough, a Mayor and local grandee on Teesside. The family's fortune was built by her grandfather, industrialist Sir Isaac Lowthian Bell MP, and Gertrude's younger years were spent alternating between her grand family home in Redcar, and the Bells' London residence in fashionable Sloane Street. Gertrude's strong connections with the North East, and her close relationship with her father (her mother died when she was just three years old) helped forge her strong, independent character. With the backing of her father and stepmother, she became a brilliant scholar and linguist – she could speak eight languages, including fluent Arabic. She went to Oxford University at the age of just seventeen, and after two years of study became the first woman to qualify for a First Class degree in Modern History at Oxford University, although women were not actually permitted to receive their degrees at a graduation ceremony at that time.

Gertrude's achievements as a pioneering woman were considerable, at a time when the 'proper' concern of young girls was deemed to be the home and family. From 1899 to 1904, she had an early career as a mountaineer, conquering both the Meije and Mont Blanc, and traced ten new paths or first ascents in the Swiss Bernese Alps. One Alpine peak is still named Gertrudspitze after her. She developed a passion for the history and culture of the Arab peoples, and her distinguished career as an archaeologist left a legacy of books, photographs, diaries and correspondence that are still valuable to scholars today. She was the only woman to hold an official position in the Arab Bureau in Cairo during World War I, and was part of the British government's diplomatic staff as a Political Officer in Basra and Oriental Secretary in Baghdad, both now in modern-day Iraq. She became the first Director of Antiquities in Iraq, and founded the Iraqi Archaeological Museum in Baghdad. In later life, she was an energetic supporter of educational development for rural communities in Iraq, and she also helped to promote Muslim women's education.

Yet Bell has never achieved the status of a 'feminist icon', even though in more recent decades many historians have been trying to put more women into the history books. Her attitudes reflected those of her own time and class, and often sit uncomfortably with twenty-first century opinions and attitudes. It may seem contradictory that in spite of her exceptional education and public career, Gertrude was a founder member of the northern branch of the Women's National Anti-Suffrage League, an organization that campaigned against votes for women before World War I. In a letter to the Times in 1908, she urged action against 'the extraordinary and regrettable programme' being pursued by the suffragettes, militant campaigners whose direct-action tactics in support of women's right to vote were becoming increasingly violent. Like many women and men of her class, Gertrude was most likely concerned that the stability of Britain and the wider Empire would be jeopardized if women were given the vote and the 'proper' order of society in which men exercised power were to be challenged. Whatever her true motivations for opposing women's voting rights, it is evident that she relished fighting for a controversial cause. In her diaries, she recorded how she loved to convert people, men and women, to the anti-suffrage side of the debate. Her letters and diaries can appear to modern eyes to be patronizing towards women (and men) of a lower class than herself, although her main concern seems to have been to judge, sometimes unfavourably, the intelligence and courage of people she met, and whether they 'measured up' to her own ideals. She greatly admired the Arab leader Faisal, whom she more than anyone manoeuvred into becoming the first king of Iraq. She also hero-worshipped her 'dear papa', with whom she had perhaps the closest and most enduring relationship in her life. She also maintained lifelong friendships with a number of women from her student days, but her difficulties in finding contentment in later life perhaps stemmed not only from the fact that she lost her 'cause' once Iraqi independence had been settled, but because few people upon closer acquaintance could live up to being idealised by her.

Like many who found their cause in times of political unrest and war, Bell did not adapt well to peace. Though no stranger to romantic love, she never married, and could neither find contentment by returning to her birth family in England, nor by settling in Baghdad. Her death in 1926, just before her 58th birthday, of an overdose of sleeping tablets, brought with it the suspicion that she had committed suicide. Whether or not this was true (and it will probably be impossible ever to say for certain), this complicated her posthumous reputation still further. In Britain, beyond the world of archaeology, it is astonishing how quickly she has been forgotten. Her diplomatic influence as an advisor to Winston Churchill and the British Government following the collapse of the Ottoman Empire after World War I is not well-known, particularly in comparison to her famous Arab Bureau contemporary, T. E. Lawrence. The fact that she does not feature at all in director David Lean's famous film Lawrence of Arabia is just one example of how notable women can be 'written out' of history. Like many women who enter the public sphere of politics, she was judged in her own day and after her death according to how she looked as much as by her intelligence and achievements. As recently as 1993, in the obituary of another great female traveller, Freya Stark, the Times gave the opinion that Stark was 'extremely feminine' while Gertrude Bell was 'a rich masculine person who *floored the pashas flat*'. A more fitting tribute was made by her friend Vita Sackville-West, who recalled Gertrude's 'irrepressible vitality' and her 'gift of making everyone feel suddenly eager, of making you feel that life was full and rich and exciting'. There is much to admire in Gertrude Bell's refusal to conform to the expectations of her day regarding 'normal' gender roles, particularly with regard to academic scholarship, exploration, politics and diplomacy. These are areas of life in the public eye which still present particular obstacles today for girls and women. It should be possible to consider for ourselves Gertrude Bell's qualities and achievements, and understand why certain attitudes have quite rightly passed into history, without condemning her for not sharing twenty-first century values.

Helen Berry

Walking the Long Road: The Love Letters of Gertrude Bell and Charles Doughty Wylie

Nowhere are the ambiguities and tensions in Gertrude Bell's life and character more evident than in her relationships, particularly with Charles Doughty-Wylie (1868–1915). It was passionate and tortured, and for both proved the defining emotional crisis of their adult lives. Yet, remarkably, in a relationship that lasted almost two years, in total they spent no more than seven days together. To an extent unthinkable today, theirs was a connection built and sustained through letters. Their extraordinary correspondence is a window onto their lives and a world sliding inexorably to war.

In the years immediately following her death, the unconventional in Gertrude Bell – her wild swings between elation and despair, her need to be taken seriously as a traveller and a scholar, and, above all, to be loved – was painstakingly sifted out by early biographers. As explorer and stateswoman, 'Queen of the Desert', she appeared forbidding and remote.

The reality, as the letters to Doughty-Wylie reveal, was very different. Caught between the strength of her own nature on the one hand and the conventions of her times on the other, throughout her life Gertrude lurched from one devastating emotional crisis to another. The pattern was set early on when, aged twenty-four, she descended on Persia and there fell in love with Henry Cadogan, secretary at the British Embassy. A rakish figure, Cadogan proposed to and was accepted by Bell, but her happiness was not shared by her family. Unwilling to defy her father, Bell broke off the engagement and returned to Britain.

Cadogan drowned shortly after her departure from Teheran, his death apparently a tragic accident.

Grieving in the immediate aftermath of Cadogan's death, Bell came to see in 'the East' something of the mystical that was lacking in industrial North-East England. She was to be drawn back repeatedly to the deserts of Arabia which, towards the end of 1913, were to provide the backdrop for her developing relationship with Charles Doughty-Wylie. Superficially, he conformed well with the ideal of the Edwardian army officer. However, though a soldier of outstanding courage, a natural leader of men, and diplomat of great tact and skill, his was a mask of command. Highly-strung and scholarly, he was prone to self-questioning fits of depression. He was also married, to Lilian, which set the difficult tone of his relationship with Gertrude. The marriage produced no children and was strained by periods of lengthy separation as Charles took up a succession of diplomatic postings in Turkey, the Balkans and Abyssinia.

Doughty-Wylie first met Bell in 1907 when she paused at the Turkish city of Konya, where he was serving as British Military Attaché. During the next six years they crossed paths only once more until, at her father's invitation, Doughty-Wylie went to stay for a weekend at Rounton Grange, the Bell family home near Northallerton. Later, when the letters that passed between them had become more than a function of enforced separation, both Charles and Gertrude would invest in this first weekend an almost mystical significance. From then on, they wrote constantly to one another. In the beginning, at least, the passion was a little one-sided. Doughty-Wylie, abroad on diplomatic missions, responded slowly, too slowly for Gertrude, and his brisk letters detailing his diplomatic work threw her into a spiral of self-doubt.

Sentimentally advanced, but conventionally repressed, Doughty-Wylie was taken aback by Bell's emotional letters. Only later, once she had embarked on her final great desert expedition in late-1913 and he was marooned in Addis Ababa as British Consul, did he lower his guard, writing initially out of loneliness. From her self-imposed desert isolation, a journey which several of her biographers have speculated was an attempt to escape from her tortured feelings for Doughty-Wylie, she dashed off notes full of joy that he, at last, reciprocated her love for him.

In March 1914 the dynamic of their relationship changed. Belatedly realising the impact his words had on Gertrude, Doughty-Wylie oscillated wildly between declarations of love and bleak statements that he could never leave his wife. Would Gertrude be content to be his mistress? For Gertrude, resting in Baghdad after a gruelling journey across what is now Saudi Arabia, this proved too much. Exhausted and depressed, over six days she wrote him an immensely-long letter. Upset and often repeating herself, she poured out her resentment and sadness. 'Had any woman such letters before?' she demanded of him. The letter proved cathartic, but she ended on a note of decision. Unconventional in so many ways, she could not, and would not, escape her upbringing. The impact on her family, and on her reputation, would be too severe. She would not be his mistress.

Their relationship continued. In January 1915, Doughty-Wylie was recalled from Abyssinia to London, pending a military posting from the War Office. Excitedly, he and Gertrude, who was by now working with the Red Cross in Boulogne, made plans to see one another. They were alone together for four days. Then Doughty-Wylie left for the Mediterranean. He had been posted to the staff of General Sir Ian Hamilton, the leader of the Mediterranean Expeditionary force and charged with storming the Gallipoli Peninsula and taking Constantinople.

Soon after arriving at Gallipoli, Doughty-Wylie was killed by a Turkish sniper whilst leading an attack on enemy positions. Armed only with a cane, numerous eyewitnesses commented later on his complete lack of fear, and his bravery was acknowledged in the posthumous award of the Victoria Cross. In his final letter to Gertrude, written on 21 April 1915 and seeking to allay her fears for his safety, he was full of confidence: 'I have a presentiment that this affair will be a brilliant success'.

His death devastated Bell. From then until her own death, she threw herself into her work. There were other infatuations, but they were fleeting by comparison. In March 1915, desolate at the thought of her life without him, she had told him that she would commit suicide should he die. His last words to her were a plea:

My dear don't (this is what weighs me down) don't do what you talked of – its horrible to me to think of – that's why I told you about my wife, – how much more for you – don't do anything so unworthy of so free and brave a spirit – one must walk along the road to the long end of it – […] You to die for whom the world holds so much! – for whom there is always the pure delight of capability and power well used – don't do it – or in some far world my ghost will be the sadder – time is nothing, we join up again – but to hurry the pace is unworthy of us after all.

David Lowther

Gertrude Bell as an Archaeologist and Explorer

Gertrude's workforce at Binbirkilise in Turkey taken during her recording of the site. Photograph by Gertrude Bell, June 1907

Gertrude Bell was brought up very much within the British establishment, but as a young woman, in spite of her family background and excellent university performance, her parents perceived Gertrude's need for further education, to rid her of, as her stepmother Lady Florence put it, '*her Oxfordy manner*'. They resolved to send Gertrude to stay with her aunt whose husband Sir Frank Lascelles was British Minister in Tehran. Gertrude relished the experience! Her journey to Persia via Bucharest and Constantinople began a lifetime spent immersed in other cultures made possible initially by the wealth and support of her parents.

Gertrude explored Persia on horseback, photographed, wrote and took lessons in Persian. Once home she published two volumes *The Divan of Hafiz* and *Persian Pictures*, a sign of times to come spent in England writing up her journeys abroad. Subsequent trips with her father and brother took her around the world as far afield as India, Burma, Singapore, Japan and Canada, but for much of the period until well into her forties when war broke out Gertrude was to journey in the Ottoman Empire. Travelling developed Gertrude's love of history, an interest in buildings and narratives of past empires which informed, and were informed by, her understanding of the present.

Her peripatetic life among others able to travel systematically integrated Gertrude Bell into a network of influential contacts. In 1899, for example, travelling in Greece with her father Hugh, Gertrude visited D.G. Hogarth, the brother of her university friend Janet. He was Director of the British School in Athens; an archaeologist with whom she was later to work in Cairo for British Military Intelligence.

At the age of thirty-one, in 1900, during her seven-month stay based in Jerusalem, Gertrude took lessons in Arabic and exploring with increasing independence visited ancient sites such as Palmyra, Aleppo, Petra, Mshatta and Qasr Amra. Her careful documentation of this trip in more than 500 photographs reveals a growing love of archaeology and interest in the people of the

region. Those images remain of considerable international significance. Far from holiday snaps, her photographs increasingly represented a disciplined inventory of her travels - consciously created to record places as they stood in 1900. They were to become a source of inspiration for her travel writing and her own archaeological work. But they now form part of an internationally recognised archive that, complemented by her letters and diaries, continually takes on new significance, especially when buildings are damaged or destroyed.

This significance became apparent, for example, almost as soon as Bell photographed the desert palace at Mshatta, when in 1903 its main gate was transported to Berlin as a gift from the Ottoman Sultan to the Kaiser of Germany. Although then inexperienced in archaeology, in November 1904, Bell spent time in Paris tutored by Salomon Reinach, editor of the academic journal *Revue Archéologique* who seized on the idea that Bell should write a review article of the academic publication of Mshatta. Bell's rather sycophantic evaluation of the work by the now infamous art historian Josef Strzygowski which as it turned out had considerable methodological flaws, helped to establish her within the network of international scholars of medieval architecture.

Bell worked hard to acquire the skills employed by archaeologists to document attributes of buildings in detail. In 1906 and 1907, she published churches encountered on a journey made in 1905 from Syria along the coast of Turkey and then onto the Anatolian plateau, where she visited Binbirkilise (Turkish for Thousand and One Churches). This was a site of interest to the famous Historical Geographer and New Testament Scholar Sir William Ramsay whom by chance she met at nearby Konya. How could Ramsay refuse the proposal that they return to Binbirkilise for an expedition financed by her

father? In 1907 they excavated and planned churches with a team of workmen for six weeks 'the first to put spade to soil in the interior of Asia Minor'. Her careful records became a kind of intellectual currency she shared with established academics as she traded notes and photographs. Bell continued her apparent deference to Strzygowski as an established authority but rather than using her discoveries to criticise his interpretations, she consciously and publicly cultivated her association by dedicating *The Thousand and One Churches* (1909) to him. She also privately cultivated her affections for Doughty-Wylie the British military consul she met in 1907 at Konya.

While in many ways conservative and operating within the structures of established society, Bell, as a western woman, used travel in the Middle East to achieve the extraordinary. She gained a sense of freedom and a striking identity both in the field and at home. Bell journeyed usually with her male servant Fattuh an Armenian Christian. They did not travel light. She had her own tent, bed, table, chairs and other equipment and of course, hers was a working library; volumes now in Newcastle University's Special Collections are complete with annotations scribbled in the field.

For the following years Bell courted danger to pursue her genuine fascination with early Byzantine and Islamic architecture which indirectly set her up for new roles in the future. Five 'months of suspense and even of terror' in 1909 journeying from Syria into Mesopotamia along the River Euphrates and back up the Tigris to Eastern Turkey were recounted in *Amurath to Amurath*. But she went back. Setting out from Damascus to Baghdad, in March in 1911, she finished her survey of Ukhaidir an early Islamic desert palace which she had discovered in 1909 and was the first to record and publish (1914). The following month she met T.E. Lawrence (of Arabia) excavating at the ancient site at Carchemish, where he was working with her old acquaintance David Hogarth.

Her most dangerous expedition was to Arabia in 1913. Following her election as fellow to the Royal Geographical Society in London, where she was trained in surveying techniques, she journeyed to Hail in Arabia, giving her a unique knowledge of what was to become within a few months a strategic part of the world.

Bell's journeys became pathways for developing her identity and status through which she forged new relationships. The knowledge and skills acquired equipped her to serve in the uncertain times during World War I and its aftermath. Recognised in 1918 by The Royal Geographical Society Founder's Medal 'For her important explorations and travels in Asia Minor, Syria, Arabia and on the Euphrates', the legacy of her journeys continues to hold international significance.

Mark Jackson

Top: *Gertrude Bell's pack horses and men crossing a brushwood bridge over Wadi Muhammadi, Iraq. Photograph by Gertrude Bell, February 1911.*
Right: *The gateway at Mshatta, which is now in the Pergamon Museum in Berlin. Photograph by Gertrude Bell, March 1900.*

Gertrude Bell and the First World War

The First World War was the catalyst for a new direction in Gertrude Bell's life. In early 1914, shortly before the outbreak of war, Gertrude returned from her journey to Hail. This expedition established her expertise in Arabia and resulted in the most recent knowledge of the territory available to the British. Combined with her extensive knowledge of Ottoman lands gathered on her earlier archaeological journeys, together with the network of contacts built up over decades, Gertrude enjoyed a better understanding of the various ethnic and religious groups than most in the British establishment. Well versed in operating within the upper echelons of British society, Gertrude had also spent much of her adult life interacting with the small network of British diplomats, archaeologists and other Europeans working in the Ottoman Empire. She was ideally placed to serve British army intelligence after war broke out.

In November 1914, following the outbreak of the First World War, Gertrude was sent for by the Red Cross to work in their Boulogne office, helping to trace missing and wounded soldiers. Upon her arrival, Gertrude was faced with a chaotic and ineffectual system for recording the missing and wounded. She took it upon herself to reorganise the office, and to put in place new indexing systems. Gertrude felt strongly that the Red Cross should be sensitive when informing families of the loss of their sons, fathers and brothers, and explained this to her mother: 'I think the form in which news is conveyed is one of the most important points in our work [...] It's enough that people should learn that the man is dead without hearing the terrible things that I know.' (12 January 1915).

In March 1915, Gertrude agreed to move to the London headquarters of the Red Cross, to continue her work recording missing and wounded soldiers, and informing their families. By November 1915, however, after less than four months at the British Red Cross HQ, David Hogarth, who had known Gertrude since 1899, enlisted her to come and work at the newly established Arab Bureau in Cairo, a British intelligence organisation dealing with Middle Eastern affairs. T.E. Lawrence – better known as Lawrence of Arabia – also worked for the Bureau and the two became close friends. Gertrude was employed by the Bureau to interpret reports from Central Arabia, as well as to document Arab tribes, their numbers and lineage.

In late January 1916, Gertrude went to Delhi to meet the Viceroy of India, Lord Charles Hardinge. She was to discuss the friction between the British Intelligence Departments of India and Egypt over the 'Arab Question', and to communicate the views of her department. Initially unsure of the success of this plan, her visit to Delhi was in fact extremely productive, and led to her being sent by the Viceroy to Basra in Mesopotamia in order to help with the Intelligence Department there, but also to improve communication between the different departments by acting as liaison between them.

When Gertrude arrived in Basra in March 1916, she gave her full attention to a number of tasks, which included classifying tribal material, a process in which her own prior knowledge from her travels was, according to Gertrude, 'very handy in many ways'. Gertrude also had strong views on the political situation in the Middle East, and was frustrated with what she perceived to be Britain's mishandling of it:

We rushed into the business with our usual disregard for a comprehensive political scheme. We treated Mesop[otamia] as if it were an isolated unit, instead of which it is part of Arabia, its politics indissolubly connected with the great and far reaching Arab question, which presents indeed, different facets as you regard it from different aspects, and is yet always and always one and the same indivisible block. (29 April 1916).

In June 1916, Gertrude was appointed to the paid position of Official Correspondent to Cairo, and also head of the Iraq branch of the Arab Bureau as an officer of the Indian Expeditionary Force D. She became increasingly influential, providing the Intelligence Department with summaries of recent Arabian history, and writing memoranda about British-Arabian relations, for example, 'The Nomad Tribes of Arabia'. Anonymously authoring a well-received text, *The Arab of Mesopotamia*, Gertrude was later amused by reviews of the book that assumed it had been written by a group of 'practical men', writing to her mother, 'Why yes of course I wrote all the *Arab of Mesopotamia*. I've loved the reviews which speak of the practical men who were the anonymous authors etc. It's fun being practical men isn't it' (5 September 1918) She was suitably humble about her work in her letters home, but also acknowledged the limitations placed upon her by her gender, commenting that 'One can't do much more than sit and record if one is of my sex'.

Gertrude left Basra for Baghdad in April 1917, following the British occupation of Baghdad on 11 March 1917. Gertrude arrived in Baghdad on 20 April 1917 to join Sir Percy Cox in the new British administration. Her duties were again wide-ranging – as well as writing articles for the War Office, she took on as many jobs as she could. In October 1917, Gertrude was awarded a CBE for her war work, though she displayed a characteristic lack of excitement to the news, writing to her father that such awards 'mean so very little and I never can manage to remember who has got them and who hasn't' (2 November 1917). Instead, she preferred to focus on her work, which included an appointment as editor of *Al Arab*.

Gertrude was passionate about the future of Iraq, and wanted to ensure that the best was done for both the country and its people, writing to her parents in May 1917 that 'I don't think I shall ever be able to detach myself permanently from the fortunes of this country'. On 30 October 1918, eleven days before the ceasefire of the First World War, the Turkish government signed the Armistice of Mudros with the Allied Forces. On 1 November 1918, Gertrude wrote to her mother, 'Today war has ceased here – the official announcement of the Turkish armistice has reached us. It's almost more than one can believe'. However, Gertrude's work only intensified in the months following the end of the war. She was heavily involved in decision-making regarding Iraq, and while she felt strongly that the British administration needed to act in the best interests of the Iraqi population, she also had her own very clear ideas about what those best interests were. She was, for example, frustrated with calls for an Arab Amir to lead the country instead of Sir Percy Cox. For Gertrude, the only viable option in January 1919 was British rule in the Middle East:

The East is inclined to lose its head over the promise of settling for itself what is to become of it. It can't settle for itself really – we out here know that very well – because it might hit on something that certainly wouldn't imply stable government and that we can't allow in the interests of universal peace. (10 January 1919).

In the years following the end of the First World War, the British Government's attentions turned to determining the borders of the new Iraq, and Gertrude was heavily involved in the decision-making process regarding this. In 1919, she attended the Paris Peace Conference as the representative of the Arab Bureau, and in March 1921, attended the Cairo Conference, organised by Winston Churchill with the objective to work towards an independent Arab Government. To that end, Bell was instrumental in the selection of Prince Faisal as the new King of Mesopotamia, who was crowned in July 1921. Perhaps most famously, however, Bell was central in drawing the borders of Iraq during this period. In a letter to her father of December 1921, she writes, rather casually, 'I had a well spent morning at the office making out the Southern desert frontier of the Iraq [...]. One way and another, I think I've succeeded in compiling a reasonable frontier'. After the coronation of King Faisal, the drawing of these borders, and the establishment of the

new Iraqi Government, Bell refocused her efforts into preserving the archaeology of the new state, and in October 1922 was appointed the Honorary Director of Antiquities for Iraq. The extent of Bell's involvement in reshaping the Middle East following the First World War and the creation of Iraq continues to be powerfully felt today.

Mark Jackson and Emma Short

Gertrude Bell and T.E. Lawrence during the Cairo conference, 1921. Their influence on the discussions led to them being called the 'uncrowned potentates of Arabia'.

Coronation of Faisal in Baghdad, 1921. Gertrude Bell, holding eye glasses, can be seen amongst the British dignitaries attending the ceremony.

Al-Khatun

Gertrude Bell led a unique life, one which makes you ponder the motivation behind her extraordinary achievements. It was not fortune; for she was born into a wealthy family; nor was it fame; something Lawrence of Arabia enjoyed. A glimpse of that motivation reveals itself in the letters she wrote which, from time to time, mention her desire to become 'A Person'.

Gertrude's achievements, prior to her involvement in the formation of Iraq, reflect an urge to make a mark on history and a need to be appreciated for astounding mental and physical talents. The extreme nature of her adventures, like mountain climbing and roaming the Arabian desert, is matched by original scholarly achievements which Bell was keen to display in the form of published books and articles.

Arguably, Gertrude's most powerful mark on history is her major role in establishing the state of Iraq. She served the British Empire in carving away the land from the crumbling Ottoman Empire, but she was also serving her own personal ambition. She wrote to her stepmother with regards to this role 'I feel at times rather like the Creator about the middle of the week. He must have wondered what it was going to be like, as I do.' (5 December 1918). Could that be the reason why she wanted to stay in Iraq permanently? Was staying an act of linking her name eternally to Iraq? This is possible but there are other reasons: the way Iraqis, or at least certain circles, regarded her and made her feel: 'Light of our eyes' they said, … - I almost began to think I were a person.' (21 October 1925).

This was not how all Iraqis felt towards Bell, though. The way she was (and is still perceived) reveals a complex web of differing perspectives; matched only by the complexity of Bell's own multifaceted personality.

Attitudes towards Bell: Admiration

In Iraq, Gertrude Bell was addressed by people of different backgrounds as Khatun. A khatun is a noble lady of high reverence. In Arabic, the prefix 'Al' means 'The'. In a short time people started referring to her as Al-Khatun.

She expressed her excitement to her parents through her letters. Most notable is the title Umm Al-Muminin: 'Darling, do you know what they call me here? Umm al Mumium, the Mother of the Faithful, and the last person who bore that name was Ayeshah, the wife of the Prophet. Isn't it beloved of them! But you see why I can't leave.' (7 December 1921). Another title she had was 'Ukhti' or 'my sister', which is how King Faisal I addressed her. She proudly wrote to her father describing an important meeting with Fahad Beg (the paramount chief of the Anizah tribe) and another tribal leader from Hail – in which the Southern border of Iraq was being established. When Kinahan Cornwallis, who was an advisor to the Iraqi King Faisal, asked Fahad Beg to define his tribal dominion, he simply replied: 'You ask the Khatun. She knows.' (5 December 1915). She had the recognition and trust of some of the most powerful men in Iraq.

Attitudes towards Bell: A Different Perspective

Not all Iraqis trusted Gertrude Bell. She was, and still is, often referred to as 'The Spy'. She was the face of the British Mandate which most Iraqis rejected. Suspicions regarding her political motives were exacerbated after the publication of her letters following her death. The translation of those letters appeared in the political

Right: One of Gertrude's Alpine guides on an ice peak in Switzerland, 1901.

newspaper *Al-Bilad*. There was anger against some of her remarks, especially her criticism of religious figures. Also, she identified people in her letters as Sunni, Shia, Kurds, and so on; a divisive rhetoric especially considering how she favoured the inclusion of personnel from one sect in the new government over the others. The anger even prompted political poems against Bell including one by the prominent poet, Muhammad Mahdi Al-Jawahiri, in which he accuses Bell of deceitfulness.

Gertrude Bell's legacy in establishing the Iraqi museum is also controversial. On one hand many admire this step to preserve the rich history of Mesopotamia, while it could also be argued that the Mesopotamian heritage (which Bell mobilised as a foundation narrative for establishing a new nation) eventually became the rhetoric used by subsequent regimes to legitimise their claim to power. The centrality of this narrative is evident not only in the construction of national museums in Iraq's early years or Saddam Hussein's appropriation of archaeological sites, but also in their recent destruction by the so called ISIS in a symbolic act of crushing Iraq and its history.

A Contemporary Perspective

The unfolding events in Iraq have renewed interest in Bell's legacy. The wealth of letters and diary notes left by Bell are a rich source for researchers to examine her influence in various disciplines from politics, history, archaeology, literature and sociology. My own research explores one aspect of Gertrude Bell's vision; her impact on the architecture of the newly founded state of Iraq.

Her direct involvement in Iraq's architecture and urban planning has not been researched before. She was the force launching the career of J.M. Wilson, an architect in the British army, who rose to the post of Government Architect of Iraq. The life changing moment for Wilson was casually documented in Bell's letter: 'The C in C and I have been deep in consultation about the site of the future cantonment, considered in connection with the probably civil expansion. We walked over two sites, above and below Baghdad and town planning is our principal topic of conversation. It's very interesting. We have unearthed a capital young architect, named Wilson, a pupil of Lutyens and he prepares plans which we pore over. He is full of ideas and good ideas.' (27 December 1918).This letter also reveals that her role in shaping the built environments exceeds that of a powerful commissioning official.There have been many different views of Gertrude Bell but Whatever people thought of her, time has proven that 'Al-Khatun' was not just 'A Person'; she became the Khatun.

Sana S. Al-Naimi

View of the Ziggurat at Ur, taken by Gertrude in 1916. 'Those huge mounds lie in the desert about 8 miles S. of the Tigris….We waded through drifted sand to the highest ruin heap, a truncated pyramid of which the niched brick casing still stands.' (Letter to her father, November 23, 1916)..

The Making of Iraq's Antiquity Law and National Museum

When the state of Iraq was created under British mandate at the end of World War I, the Iraqi government and its British advisors, prompted by Gertrude Bell, were eager to commence archaeological research to help construct a new national identity. In 1922, this responsibility fell to Gertrude when King Faisal appointed her the Honorary Director of Antiquities. Given her extensive knowledge of Iraqi archaeological sites gained from a decade of travels across the Middle East, and her service after the war as British Oriental Secretary in Baghdad and as King Faisal's trusted advisor, Gertrude was ideally suited to the task.

In her new role, Gertrude Bell was given full authority to draft the first antiquities legislation for Iraq, which was mandated in the 1922 Anglo-Iraqi Treaty. As she wrote to her father: 'I got [King Faisal's] assistance for my Law of Excavations which I've compiled with the utmost care in consultation with the legal authorities. He has undertaken to push it through Council… I should then be able to run the whole thing in direct agreement with him…' (20 July 1922). The passage of the Antiquity Law in June 1924 ushered in a transitional period of archaeology in Iraq in which the state began to assume control over its archaeological heritage and lay the foundation for national archaeological institutions. The new legislation regulated excavations, and the sale and export of antiquities in a bid to lessen illicit looting of artefacts, which had gone unchecked prior to World War I. The most controversial provision of the law called for the partition of antiquities between foreign expeditions and the Iraqi state. As a standard clause in antiquities legislation in Middle Eastern states, Gertrude believed it was necessary to attract foreign excavations to Iraq.

Under the new Law of Antiquities, Gertrude was responsible for approving foreign archaeological missions. Determined to ensure that excavations adhered to modern systematic and scientific standards, Gertrude spent much of her time accompanying the teams to site and monitoring their progress. At the end of each field season she was also responsible for negotiating the division of antiquities with the archaeologists so that both the expedition and the Iraqi state received a representative share of the finds. Though Gertrude had the legal authority to claim the most important discoveries on behalf of the Iraqi government, her personal letters intimated that she was divided between her ties to England and her obligations to Iraq. In a letter home, she reflected: 'It's a difficult and rather agonising job, you know. We sat with our catalogues and ticked the things off… In my capacity as Director of Antiquities I'm an Iraqi official and bound by the terms on which we gave the permit for excavation' (6 March 1924).

Yet Gertrude was also eager to accommodate foreign archaeologists whose discoveries contributed to the growing Iraqi archaeological collection. In order to keep the antiquities in Iraq, Gertrude housed them in a modest room of a government building in Baghdad, but aspired

Left: *Gertrude Bell, Leonard Woolley and other European archaeologists at Ur in Iraq.*
Below: *Gertrude Bell and Leonard Woolley dividing finds at Ur in Iraq.*

to build the collection into a national museum. 'When I come back from Ur, where I am going next week for the division of the objects found this year,' she wrote to her father, 'I shall be able to begin getting in to [the collection], I hope. I shall take great pride in making it something like a real museum' (3 March 1926).

Indeed, many archaeologists privately felt Gertrude was favourable towards foreign expeditions, which encouraged archaeological research in Iraq during the early 1920s. Archaeologists from the United States and the United Kingdom, backed by wealthy American patrons seeking to authenticate the stories of the Bible, flocked to Iraq. Perhaps the most celebrated excavation during Gertrude's tenure was Sir Leonard Woolley's discovery of the royal cemetery of Ur. On the southern bank of the Euphrates River, Woolley uncovered an extraordinary array of crowns, jewellery and royal furnishings, which were later divided amongst the British Museum, the University of Pennsylvania Museum of Archaeology and Anthropology and the Baghdad Museum. Around the same time, French excavations unearthed a Sumerian palace at Kish and a German team started excavations at Warka, leading to the discovery of the celebrated Warka Vase.

As the collection began to overflow with antiquities yielded from the foreign archaeological expeditions at Assyrian, Babylonian and Sumerian sites, Gertrude successfully lobbied the Iraqi cabinet for a new building and funds to expand the museum. In 1926, the Iraq Museum was established in a building on the east bank of the Tigris River. As the new director, Gertrude dedicated her efforts to the Iraq museum, and was involved with virtually all aspects of its operation, including cataloguing and conserving new collections, and overseeing alterations and repairs to the building. Writing to her father, she confessed: 'My duty to the museum is of the first importance' (12 May 1926).

When King Faisal opened a portion of the new museum to the public in June 1926, the Iraq Museum was brimming with thousands of archaeological discoveries dating to the country's pre-Islamic past. Gertrude remained the director of the museum until her untimely death in Baghdad in July of that year. In one of the last letter's to her family, she revealed, 'I always feel, when I'm back to archaeology, that I am nothing better than an antiquarian at heart' (3 March 1926). Accordingly, in her will, she bequeathed £50,000 to the museum to continue her vision, and a wing of the museum was posthumously named in her honor.

Ninety years after the opening of the Iraq Museum and Gertrude Bell's death, the museum is widely credited as her crowning achievement. The result of the extensive archaeological explorations authorised under Bell's Antiquity Law greatly contributed to knowledge of the ancient Mesopotamian civilisation and helped build the museum into one of the most renowned in the Middle East. Despite the ongoing political instability in Iraq, today the museum stands as a testament to the enduring role Gertrude Bell played in promoting the country's archaeological heritage during the formative years of the Iraqi nation.

J. E. D. Meharry

Gertrude Bell and the Ancient City of Ur (Tell al Muqayyar)

In 1916 Gertrude Bell made her first visit to the great mounds of Ur, the Sumerian city of the moon-god Nanna, where more than 200,000 people resided at its peak. Tell al-Muqayyar ('mound of pitch'), the Arabic name of the site of the ancient city of Ur in Southern Iraq, was first described in 1625 by Pietro della Valle, a Venetian traveller, who brought back with him bricks and cylinder seals and commented on their inscriptions, noting their characteristic appearance that looked like stars and wedges (what later became known as cuneiform writing).

During the 18th and 19th centuries several explorers visited the site. William Kennett Loftus provided an early illustration of the ziggurat (the pyramid-like temple of Mesopotamia) and arbitrary excavations took place in 1853–1854 at the ziggurat by J. E. Taylor, the British vice-consul at Basra, which brought to light foundation cylinders of the Neo-Babylonian period enabling the decipherer of cuneiform Henry Rawlinson to identify the site with Ur. After the end of World War I, Reginald Campbell Thomson, the British Army's military archaeologist, excavated at the ziggurat for a few days, while H. R. Hall excavated there for three months unearthing parts of the Ehursag, the so-called Palace of Ur-Nammu, the first king of the Third Dynasty of Ur (2112–2004 BCE), and the Neo-Babylonian temenos (sacred enclosure) of Nebuchadnezzar (605–562 BCE). Though excavations ceased in 1919, they were restarted in 1922 at the request of Gertrude Bell, the Honorary Director of Antiquities in Iraq, funded by the British Museum and the University Museum of Pennsylvania and under the direction of the renowned British archaeologist Sir Leonard Woolley.

Woolley's archaeological discoveries at Ur (1922–1934) were fascinating. In twelve seasons Woolley completely unearthed the ziggurat and the entire temenos area. He also excavated parts of the residential and commercial quarters of the city. Undeniably, the most spectacular discovery was that of the Royal Cemetery, dating from about 2600 BCE, which was unearthed during four seasons, and exposed more than 1,800 graves, seventeen of which were very richly furnished. In 1934, Woolley's expedition ended and in 1935, Woolley was knighted for his outstanding contribution to archaeology.

Gertrude Bell was interested in Ur as early as 1916:

I've just had a telegram from the General at Nasiriyah, who is a friend of mine, asking me to come there on Sunday, by rail! I think I shall go for a couple of days, if only to take a railway journey. Also I have some jobs to do there. And I like General Brooking. One motors the last lap – it would be rather amusing. The ostensible object of my visit is to go out and see the great mounds of Ur of the Chaldees which I have been protecting from the ravages of Generals and railway engineers.(16 November 1916)

The fact that Leonard Woolley became the Director of Excavations made it much more pleasant to her, since she sincerely respected him. In one of her letters she wrote about him and her new role as Director of Antiquities:

I've been figuring in my capacity as Director of Archaeology. Mr Woolley arrived on Sunday - I knew him first when he was digging at Carchemish [Barak (Karkemis)], and next as Intelligence Officer at Port Sa'id [Port Said] in 1915. He's a tiresome little man but a first class digger and an archaeologist after my own heart - ie he entirely backs me up in the way I'm conducting the Department. He has come out as head of a joint expedition organized by the British Museum and Pennsylvania University and they are going to dig Ur, no less, and are prepared to put in two years' work. He came to see me on Sunday afternoon to discuss arrangements and next day I sent him round to my minister, Sabih Beg, and made an appointment for him with the King. (1 November 1922)

Gertrude Bell was very much involved in the excavations at Ur. Woolley's were amongst the earliest excavations under the new 1924 Antiquities Law of the newly founded nation of Iraq, for the drafting of which Bell was instrumental. Article 22 postulated that all finds from foreign archaeological expeditions were to be divided between Iraq and the institutions that funded the excavations. This practice became known as the Division of Archaeological Finds, and Ur was one of the first excavations where this was endorsed: the finds from Woolley's excavations were split between the nation of Iraq and the Iraq National Museum (represented by Gertrude Bell), the British Museum, and the University Museum of Pennsylvania. Every year at the close of the excavations Gertrude Bell travelled to Ur to check their progress and split the finds:

The excavations this year, without being quite so sensationally exciting as they were last year, have been extremely good and there were some wonderful objects to divide. The division was rather difficult but I think J.M. and I were very fair and reasonable — I hope Mr Woolley thinks the same in his heart, though he fussed a little, or rather declared himself to be very sad afterwards. I had one night at Ur between two bad nights in the train, but it was a very good night — it was so peaceful and restful out there in the desert. (4 March 1925)

Arguably, the motivating factor for Western countries to fund archaeological expeditions in Iraq and elsewhere at the time was the filling of their museums' cabinets. In this respect Leonard Woolley can be seen to represent the interests of the British Museum and University Museum of Pennsylvania to which the share of the finds was allocated. On the other hand, Bell was acting on behalf of Iraq, although it seems difficult to regard her as completely impartial to the British colonial interests. Nevertheless, all foreign archaeologists in Iraq recognized Bell's love for Iraq's cultural heritage and her attempts to preserve it. Leonard Woolley wrote in her obituary: 'Her ambition was to make the museum worthy of the great history of Iraq and essential to the study of its past, and the fulfillment of that ambition would be the best material monument to her', while Max Mallowan wrote: 'No tigress could have safeguarded Iraq's rights better.'

Christina Tsouparopoulou

Nimrud. Man beside upper torso and head of statue. 'So up to Tell Nimrud with Sheikh Askar of the Jebur. A pitiful sight with the inscrips. winged genii and statue standing half out of the ground' (Diary 27 April 1909). Gertrude's shock at seeing the state of the site at Nimrud shows her concern for the archaeology of Iraq as early as 1909.

The Looting of the Iraq National Museum

When Gertrude Bell was creating the National Museum in Iraq it would have been very unlikely that she even remotely contemplated the catastrophic events that were to beset her museum or the wider archaeological record of Iraq that have happened in recent years. When the monarchy that she had so carefully helped to create in 1921 was replaced finally by the dictatorship of Saddam Hussein in 1979 the ancient past found an equally, if not greater, supporter as the new President moved to paper over more recent social and religious differences in Iraq by appealing to the heritage of ancient civilisations as a unifying focus for the modern state. While many specialists complained of the quality of work and legitimacy of interpretation, archaeological sites were reconstructed, actors dressed as soldiers from earlier civilizations became common sights at national parades, and looters were punished by death. Iraq had developed a professional and dedicated State Board of Antiquities the staff of which were some of the most highly trained in the region and all looked fairly positive.

Iraq's 1991 invasion of Kuwait changed the situation dramatically. In the chaos and confusion that followed Operation Desert Storm and Iraq's overwhelming defeat by the international coalition the National Museum and all regional museums were targeted by looters and the endemic looting of archaeological sites saw a depressing spike of activity. The sanctions, and travel restrictions, that were then imposed isolated the staff of the State Board of Antiquities from their international colleagues and critical conservation chemicals and other materials were denied them. Sadly, things were only to get worse.

The failure of the USA/UK led Coalition, which invaded Iraq in 2003, to protect the museums, libraries, archives, galleries, and archaeological sites has been documented and discussed widely. Suffice to say that no attention appears to have been taken with respect to the protection of cultural property (or indeed to culture at all) during the planning for the invasion; the Coalition was taken aback by its 'catastrophic success' (a term developed in the UK MoD in the summer of 2003) and the troops who entered Baghdad in April 2003 did not even have the National Museum marked on their maps. It may be that the officer in charge of the American tank column really did make the 'militarily wrong but culturally brilliant' decision to withdraw rather than engage the Iraqi troops firing at them from the National Museum but his decision was taken out of any 'Rules of Engagement' as no rules included any reference to cultural property at all.

The looting of the National Museum, however, that took place over the 10 to 16 April, and that was mirrored at all of the regional museums, was multifaceted and complex. Much of the looting was predicated on the fact that the museums were Government institutions and therefore legitimate targets for disaffected members of the population keen to lash-out at any manifestation of Saddam's regime. Every single office of the National Museum's administration block was looted, not for antiquities, but for computers, air conditioning units, and general office furniture. In the Museum itself much of the paper-based catalogue appears to have been ransacked by those uninterested in antiquities but desperate for information of 'disappeared' friends and relations. Handfuls of files that only related to irrelevant ancient artefacts were thus discarded, kicked around the floor, and

Left: *Plaque in the Iraq National Museum Baghdad, honouring Gertrude Bell as the founder of the Museum.*
Below: *Unveiling of the bust and plaque.*

lost. When looters who were actually interested in stealing ancient artefacts arrived in the galleries they were met with largely empty spaces. The only ancient objects remaining being those too large and/or heavy to move without drawing attention to activity that had been explicitly disallowed by order of Saddam Hussein. The Museum staff had moved as much of the collections as possible to safe locations. This extremely courageous act, in defiance of the regime, has largely gone without comment. Had the Museum's staff not taken this action, much more may well have been lost. Of course, some 15,000 artefacts were looted, mainly from the storerooms, of which some 8,000 remain unaccounted for.

The real catastrophe of Iraq's heritage is perhaps however, not the looting of the museums nor the burning of library and archive collections, but the looting of archaeological sites across the country. We have some understanding of what had been in the museums and other institutions, much of which had been studied and published. What we have almost no idea about is what has been illegally dug out of archaeological sites. We can only assume that most of this material is going to be, or already has been, sold as part of the illicit trade in such antiquities. This is a catastrophic loss to our understanding of the past as, even if we were to retrieve it all tomorrow, its archaeological context has been lost, thus removing ninety per cent or more of its value in helping us paint a picture of the past.

Why did all of this happen? Why was Bell's careful creation of the museums and other institutions so badly let down? Much blame can, and should, be levelled at those who planned the invasion and who ignored the importance of the culture and cultural property of Iraq. Our political leadership has failed to accept its international responsibilities. Shamefully, despite annual promises since 2004 to do so, the UK has still failed to ratify the 1954 Hague Convention on the Protection of Cultural Property in the Event of Armed Conflict and its two Protocols – the primary international humanitarian law dealing with this issue. Perhaps equally at fault however, was the heritage community who had allowed the close relationship with the military evidenced by the existence of the Monuments and Fine Arts teams in Allied armies during the Second World War to wither on the vine and disappear.

Since 2003 a small group of heritage professionals have been working to rebuild this relationship. Trust has been difficult and slow to build on both sides but over the last few years considerable progress has been made. The Blue Shield, currently an entirely voluntary organisation but frequently referred to as the 'cultural equivalent of the Red Cross', has produced a series of lists of cultural property for Iraq, Syria, Libya, and Mali that have been accepted by the military and added to their so-called 'no-strike' lists that includes education establishments, hospitals, and religious buildings. Following publication of an article suggesting a four-tier approach to military/heritage liaison the British Army is in process of rekindling the Monuments and Fine Arts team. NATO is currently funding a project that should result in an organisation-wide cultural property protection doctrine. NATO's Civilian/Military Centre of Excellence has just published a short booklet entitled *Cultural Property Protection Makes Sense* – written by those in uniform for those in uniform. Equally encouraging, the UK Government has just announced the creation of a Cultural Property Fund with funding guaranteed until 2020. I believe Gertrude Bell would have been appalled by the damage and destruction done in Iraq and more widely in Africa and the Middle East. I hope she would have welcomed these efforts, however small and however late.

Peter Stone

An American tank outside the main entrance to the looted Iraqi National Museum, April 2003. © *Joanne Farchakh Bajjaly.*

A group including Winston Churchill, Gertrude Bell and T.E. Lawrence on camels in front of the Sphinx and Pyramids during the Cairo Conference, 1921.

Gertrude Bell in Her Time and Ours

House of Commons, 12 February 2015, Destruction [and Looting] of Historic Sites (Syria and Iraq)

Tim Loughton (East Worthing and Shoreham) (Con): This debate is timely. We are about to see the release of a film about the amazing life of Gertrude Bell [*Queen of the Desert*]. Bell was an extraordinary individual who played a part in the Cairo conference in 1921, alongside Winston Churchill and T. E. Lawrence. She was part of those who created the constitution of Iraq and she was also responsible for the founding of the museum of Baghdad in 1926, the major hall of which is devoted to her memory. What happened in the 1920s sowed the seeds of what we are reaping now—what has happened in recent decades in Iraq and the greater middle east, and the history that produced Saddam Hussein […]

Robert Jenrick (Newark) (Con): I thank my hon. Friend, sitting at whose feet was like receiving a history lesson from a professor. He is the Gertrude Bell of the House of Commons

For all Britain's long history of parliamentary democracy, women were excluded until 1918, and were not on the same terms as men until 1958. Prominent where the social overlapped with the political, whether as Conservatives (Souls), Liberals (Asquithians) or Socialists (Bloomsbury), they could only be as private citizens. Gertrude Bell did not need to be in Parliament to be present in its counsels: her curious mix of internationalism and imperialism informed British foreign policy – the disastrous as well as the merely unsatisfactory – both in her time and in ours. William Ormsby-Gore, in the Commons in 1921, and Charles Cripps, in the Lords in 1928, lauded Bell's work, while 'those who have the honour of the lady's acquaintance', Ralph Glynn told MPs in 1922 'will know her great power among the Arab people', yet the Iraqi revolt meant that despite her 'education of the Arabs' the 'whole of Islam at the moment is on the move'. The measure of this 'pernicious' force was that it 'is counteracting the work which has been done by Miss Bell', who inevitably became known as the 'female Lawrence of Arabia'.

Only four years later however it fell to that arch imperialist Leo Amery, as Colonial Secretary, to announce: 'I greatly regret to inform the House, to many of whose Members she was personally well known' that Bell had died in Baghdad, her death 'hastened by many years of unsparing work in a trying climate'. Britain had 'lost not only a most valuable public servant, but also a remarkable and indeed unique personality' whose 'intimate knowledge of the East enabled her to render exceptional service to the British Forces' and 'profound sympathy with the Arab people and her strong faith in their future, played no small part in shaping the policy of mutual confidence and co-operation' which led to the state of

Iraq. 'In one sense at least she was thus happy in the moment of her death.'

Bell's parliamentary presence was greater in death. In 1943, parrying Nancy Astor in the Commons, Harold Nicolson cited Bell as a reason for liberalising the Diplomatic Service, hitherto barred to women: 'there are many occasions when it would be very much in the public interest to appoint some well-known woman – known for her probity, intelligence, ability and balance – to some diplomatic post.' Moreover, he wanted permanent female attachés 'who would devote their very special gifts to the study of women's interests in those countries'. Bell may have approved, but the proper 'feminisation' of both the service and foreign policy had to wait for Judith Hart and Barbara Castle. In the aftermath of another ill-fated British endeavour in the region, George Wigg MP revealed 'I was introduced to the subject of Islam through the medium of [this] great woman. She often talked to me about the impact of Western civilisation upon the Arab peoples, and spoke in contemptuous terms of Europeans who came to Baghdad in a mood of Western superiority'. Then came 'Suez'. 'One day in the late autumn of 1956 we saw all that Gertrude Bell and Lawrence stood for thrown away.'

Wigg was keen to point out that not only did he know Bell but he went to her funeral; his colleague Tam Dalyell did neither, but in 2003 when opposing 'Tony Blair's Suez' gave as evidence of the merit of his insights that Bell knew his father. Shortly after the US legislature passed a 'Joint Resolution to Authorize the Use of United States Armed Forces Against Iraq', Lord Selsdon quoted Bell in the UK legislature to not treat Iraq 'as if it were an isolated political unit, instead of which it is part of Arabia, its politics indissolubly connected with the great and far reaching Arab question'. 'There is no peace to be imposed from outside … Let us learn from our errors', soon to be Foreign Office minister Lord Howell intoned in 2008; he ended with the words of Gertrude Bell: 'Oh, if we can make them work together, and find their own salvation for themselves, what a fine thing that would be'. That says it all.'

Bell was held responsible for Iraq and Syria in the next century. In 2002 the historian Lord [Hugh Thomas rued her dissuading Churchill at Cairo from establishing an independent Kurdistan, and in 2014 the interventionist former Defence Secretary Lord [Tom] King regretted the press republishing 'the unhelpful comment of Gertrude Bell about the people in the region' that 'No one knows exactly what they do want, least of all themselves, except that they don't want us'. Supporting the Assad regime in Damascus in 2009, Richard Spring MP espoused Syria's history of 'invasions and occupiers' about which Bell wrote 'with amazement in her diaries'; when, three years later, the regime reacted repressively to protest movements, Lord Risby despaired at the reversal of Syria's 'exceptional tradition of religious co-existence.' After all, 'Gertrude Bell wrote about it.'

What would most survive of Gertrude Bell was culture. In 2003, Lord Avebury said it was because of that 'brilliant citizen of this country, who … excavated many of the important sites' and 'started the Department of Antiquities' that Britain had a responsibility in helping Iraq safeguard its cultural heritage. In her own country, Queen of the Desert was welcome if for no other reason than that Bell had managed in 2015 what she had not in 1962: in Lawrence of Arabia's 228 minutes and cast of thousands there was not a single woman; that Lawrence may become known as the 'male Gertrude Bell', is itself a monument of posthumous change.

Martin Farr

A Brief History of the Gertrude Bell Archive and Related Projects at Newcastle University

Several months after Gertrude Bell's death in July 1926, her father Sir Hugh Bell, then a Governor of Armstrong College, Newcastle upon Tyne, wrote to its Principal indicating that the family would like to donate Gertrude Bell's 'Oriental Library' of books to the College. In October 1926 the books and photograph albums which Gertrude had amassed were moved from the family home, Rounton Grange, to Armstrong College.

Some years later, in 1962, Gertrude's half-sister, Lady Florence Elsa Richmond donated a large tin trunk containing Gertrude Bell's letters, papers and travel diaries to the College; in 1965 the remaining letters – the Bell/Doughty-Wylie correspondence – were delivered to what was by then the University of Newcastle upon Tyne with the proviso that they were not to be opened until 1976. At that point the University was formally authorised to 'exercise all legal rights in the letters and papers'.

In the 1970s, Stephen Hill, an MPhil student in the Department of Archaeology wrote his thesis on the Early Byzantine Churches of Cilicia, using Bell's photographs and publications as a point of reference for comparison with the monuments which still existed. In addition to his thesis, Stephen organised an exhibition of Bell photographs which was first displayed in the University's Hatton Gallery and which subsequently toured nationally and internationally, and received national publicity.

Consequently, in 1976 a project funded by the Manpower Services Commission commenced in the Department of Archaeology, with the purpose of unpacking, cataloguing, preserving and reprinting the 6,000 plus photographs and negatives in the Archive. Stephen Hill managed the team of four (two researchers and two photographic technicians) who carried out the work. The archive was then housed in Special Collections in the University Library; Alistair Elliot, the Keeper of Special Collections, gave immense support to the MSC project by giving unfettered access to the Archive. Apart from the green albums containing mounted copies of her photographs, annotated with her handwritten identifications, all the other photographic materials in the archive, such as negatives and photographic notebooks, were kept in the strong room of the Library, essentially as they had arrived in the 1920s. In December 1977, the Library turned over the Gertrude Bell Photographic Archive to the Department of Archaeology which continues to manage the dissemination of the photographs to enquirers from across the world.

In addition to the identification of the photographs which was made easier by Bell's notes and the work Stephen Hill had already put into the task, the conservation work involved washing the original negatives in distilled water, making a complete set of contact prints from the negatives, storing them in acid free envelopes and finally creating a new set of 35mm negatives by photographing the contact prints.

The MSC project lasted several years and resulted in the publication of the '*Catalogue of the Gertrude Bell Photographic Archive*'.

A subsequent project to transcribe the diaries and thousands of letters in the Archive was funded by a number of organisations and institutions (British Library, British Academy, Gulbenkian Foundation, James Knott Trust, Ambassador Terence Clark, the then Ambassador to Iraq) and lasted until 1987. The purpose of this project was to conserve through copying the material and to create an index which would aid researchers. Because this project got underway in the early 1980s, before the internet was available, the initial means of transcription was a manual typewriter! Within several months of the outset of the project, a connection was made to the University's main frame computer via a crude modem and dumb terminal. This development transformed the project into one which could employ the powers of digital technology both for indexing or search purposes, but in time would enable the material to be incorporated into a website.

The arrival of the internet was the impetus for *The Gertrude Bell Project* a major digitisation project in the late 1990s lasting two years funded by JISC (Joint Information Systems Committee). *The Gertrude Bell Project* was conducted by two full-time project members who transcribed the letters and diaries for two years with the help of the work of previous projects, while a third scanned the photographs and other part-time team members identified photographs and produced the website. The website, now nearly twenty years old, has resulted in an average of over 470,560 page views per year since 2010. Both the School of History, Classics and Archaeology and the Robinson Library Special

Collections have daily requests about the archive from all over the world. There is significant interest from newspaper and radio journalists, TV producers, film makers and writers of books, magazine articles and school children who want to write about Bell, and there is also collaboration with actors, artists, museum curators and designers who want to use the images from the archive for their own work.

Between 2013 and 2015 the School of History, Classics and Archaeology has been involved in a number of initiatives to develop research and impact through the Bell Archive including collaborating with British Institute for the Study of Iraq (Gertrude Bell Memorial) BISI for 'Gertrude Bell a Life and Legacy' a major conference held at the Royal Society and British Academy, London; running a Facebook page and Twitter account to generate discussion about Gertrude Bell; working with the Robinson Library to upload nearly seven hundred largely unseen scans of Personalia online, and producing learning resources for School children as well as co-curating the 2016 exhibition at the Great North Museum: Hancock '*The Extraordinary Gertrude Bell*'. You can visit the Gertrude Bell Archive at www.gerty.ncl.ac.uk.

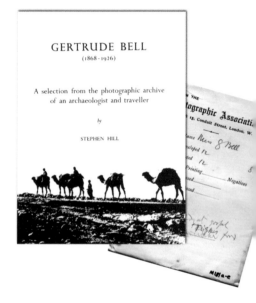

Lynn Ritchie and Mark Jackson
(with contributions from Stephen Hill and Jim Crow)

List of Contributors

Sana S. Al-Naimi, PhD Candidate, School of Architecture, Planning and Landscape, Newcastle University

Susan Beaumont, PhD Candidate in History, School of History, Classics and Archaeology, Newcastle University

Prof Helen Berry, Dean of Postgraduate Studies, School of History, Classics and Archaeology, Newcastle University

Dr Martin Farr, Senior Lecturer in History, School of History, Classics and Archaeology, Newcastle University

Dr Mark Jackson, Lecturer in Archaeology and Manager of the Gertrude Bell Photographic Archive, School of History, Classics and Archaeology, Newcastle University

David Lowther, PhD Candidate in History, School of History, Classics and Archaeology, Newcastle University

Eva Meharry, PhD Candidate, Division of Archaeology, University of Cambridge

Andrew Parkin, Keeper of Archaeology, Great North Museum: Hancock, Newcastle upon Tyne and Guest Member of Staff, School of History, Classics and Archaeology, Newcastle University

Lynn Ritchie, Independent researcher, former Research Assistant Dept. of Archaeology, Newcastle University

Dr Emma Short, Research Associate, School of English Literature, Languages and Linguistics, Newcastle University

Prof Peter Stone OBE, Professor of Heritage Studies, Head of School, School of Arts and Cultures, Newcastle University

Dr Christina Tsouparopoulou, Researcher, Visiting Lecturer, School of History, Classics and Archaeology, Newcastle University

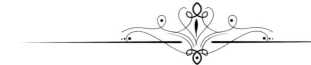